FUN FACT FILE: WORLD WONDERS!

20 FUN FACTS ABOUT STONEHENGE

By Michael Sabatino

Gareth Stevens
Publishing

Please visit our website, www.garethstevens.com. For a free color catalog of all our high-quality books, call toll free 1-800-542-2595 or fax 1-877-542-2596.

Library of Congress Cataloging-in-Publication Data

Sabatino, Michael.
20 fun facts about Stonehenge / by Michael Sabatino.
    p. cm. — (Fun fact file: world wonders!)
Includes index.
ISBN 978-1-4824-0460-9 (pbk.)
ISBN 978-1-4824-0461-6 (6-pack)
ISBN 978-1-4824-0457-9 (library binding)
1. Stonehenge (England) — Juvenile literature. 2. Wiltshire (England) — Antiquities — Juvenile literature. 3. Megalithic monuments — England — Wiltshire — Juvenile literature. I. Title.
DA142.S23 2014
936.2—dc23
First Edition

Published in 2014 by
Gareth Stevens Publishing
111 East 14th Street, Suite 349
New York, NY 10003

Copyright © 2014 Gareth Stevens Publishing

Designer: Sarah Liddell
Editor: Greg Roza

Photo credits: Cover, p. 1 Peter Dazeley/Photographer's Choice RF/Getty Images; p. 5 Gail Johnson/Shutterstock.com; p. 6 Comstock/Comstock Images/Getty Images; pp. 7, 12 Dorling Kindersley/Dorling Kindersley/Getty Images; pp. 8–9 iStockphoto/Thinkstock.com; p. 10 Jessica Key/E+/Getty Images; p. 11 Volina/Shutterstock.com; p. 13 Xseon/Shutterstock.com; p. 14 Joshua Raif/Shutterstock.com; p. 15 DEA PICTURE LIBRARY/Contributor/De Agostini/Getty Images; p. 16 De Agostini Picture Library/Contributor/De Agostini/Getty Images; p. 17 ML Harris/The Image Bank/Getty Images; pp. 18–19 Phillip Minnis/Shutterstock.com; p. 20 Vladimir Pcholkin/Taxi/Getty Images; p. 21 Matt Cardy/Stringer/Getty Images News/Getty Images; p. 22 British Library/Robana/Contributor/Hulton Fine Art Collection/Getty images; p. 23 photo courtesy of Wikimedia Commons, Stonehenge Archer - Salisbury and South Wiltshire Museum.jpg; p. 24 photo courtesy of Wikimedia Commons, Stonehenge megalith with ancient carvings April 2005.jpg; p. 25 Bryan Busovicki/Shutterstock.com; p. 26 Hulton Archive/Stringer/Hulton Archive/Getty Images; p. 27 Matthew Brown/Flickr/Getty Images; p. 29 Image Hans Elbers/Flickr/Getty Images.

Printed in the United States of America

CPSIA compliance information: Batch #CW14GS: For further information contact Gareth Stevens, New York, New York at 1-800-542-2595.

Contents

Words in the glossary appear in **bold** type the first time they are used in the text.

Timeless Wonder

Imagine yourself standing on a grassy field early in the morning. Towering stone **structures** 18 feet (5.5 m) tall surround you. As the sun rises on this particular day, it shines through a special opening between the huge stones. You're witnessing a moment that's been shared by others for over 4,000 years: the summer **solstice** at Stonehenge.

Stonehenge, a circular stone monument built long ago, is full of mystery and folklore. For centuries, it has captured the imagination of storytellers and scientists alike.

Stonehenge stands on Salisbury Plain in Wiltshire, England.

5

FACT 1

The people who built Stonehenge are still a mystery to us.

We know very little about the people who built Stonehenge. They didn't leave any written records. However, they left behind clues. For example, **primitive** stone tools were found underground near Stonehenge. These **artifacts** tell us a little bit about the people of the time.

The builders used simple tools made of stone, wood, and animal parts to create Stonehenge.

People lived in the area long before Stonehenge was built.

Recently, researchers found the earliest known settlement in the area of Stonehenge. It existed as far back as 7500 BC. That's 5,000 years earlier than once thought. The discovery means humans lived in the area for thousands of years before Stonehenge was built.

Some settlements built around the same time as Stonehenge had a similar circular shape.

FACT 3

Stonehenge has smaller "sisters" in England and Ireland.

Though Stonehenge is the largest and most famous ancient stone monument in England, it isn't the only one. Together, England and Ireland have as many as 1,300 stone monuments. More than 170 of these are stone circles similar to Stonehenge.

Swinside Circle

A "henge" is an ancient monument built on flat land and shaped like a circle or oval. It is surrounded by ditches and a ring of earth called a bank.

Ale's Stones is an ancient stone monument in Kåseberga, Sweden. Its rocks form the outline of a ship.

Ancient stone monuments similar to Stonehenge can be found all over the world.

Stonehenge is made of megaliths—very large stones used to make ancient monuments. Stone monuments both big and small can be found in countries all over the world. The word "megalith" comes from the ancient Greek language. *Mega* means "big," and *lithos* means "stone."

FACT 5

The largest stones at Stonehenge weigh about as much as three African elephants.

The giant standing stones at Stonehenge are called sarsen stones. They're made of sandstone. Many weigh as much as 50,000 pounds (22,700 kg). The smaller stones are called bluestones. They weigh as much as 8,000 pounds (3,630 kg).

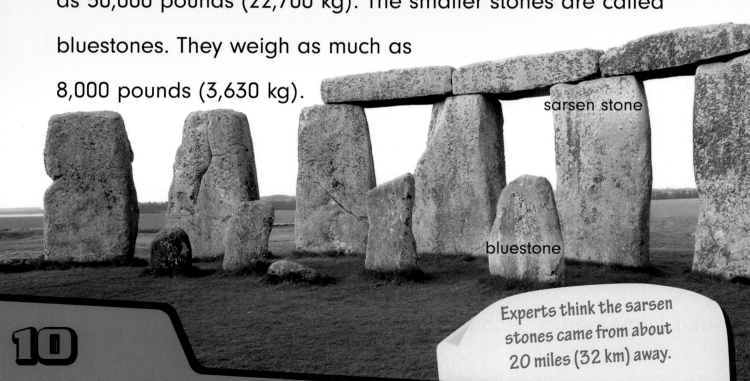

sarsen stone

bluestone

Experts think the sarsen stones came from about 20 miles (32 km) away.

FACT 6

Stonehenge's builders traveled about 160 miles (257 km) to get the bluestones.

In 2011, **geologists** announced they had found the original **quarry** for the bluestones 160 miles (257 km) away from Stonehenge. That's a long way to go when you're carrying an 8,000-pound (3,630 kg) stone! Experts used microscopes to match the stones to those in the original quarry.

The quarry for the bluestones is near a town in Wales named Pont Saeson.

FACT 7

Experts still don't know how the ancient builders brought the stones to the site.

Stonehenge's builders used primitive tools to help shape and move the stones. How they did this is still one of the great mysteries of Stonehenge. Now that we know where the bluestones came from, scientists hope they'll discover how the stones were moved.

Some experts think the stones were tied to wooden sleds, which were moved forward over rolling logs.

Some experts think the huge stones surfed on top of smaller stones to get to Stonehenge.

Man-made stone balls all about the same size were found near another henge in Scotland. Could this be a clue telling us how the megaliths were moved? Some experts think the enormous stones were set on top of these smaller stones and rolled over land.

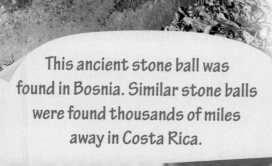

This ancient stone ball was found in Bosnia. Similar stone balls were found thousands of miles away in Costa Rica.

Perito Moreno Glacier, Argentina

FACT 9

Glaciers can move heavy stones like those at Stonehenge.

Some think there's no way people could have moved the stones. They think the stones could have been picked up by a glacier that was moving slowly over the land. When the glacier melted, it dropped the stones near Salisbury Plain.

Moving stones as large as those used to build Stonehenge is very difficult—even for modern man.

The bluestones were moved 160 miles (257 km) over land and sea to get to Salisbury Plain. In 2000, a group of people tried to make the journey using a bluestone that weighed about 3.3 tons (3 mt). They failed. The stone slipped off its boat and sunk.

These illustrations show how ancient people may have lifted the sarsen stones into place.

FACT 11

Stonehenge went through many changes during its lifetime.

The first **version** of Stonehenge was built 5,000 years ago. That's about 500 years before the Great Pyramid in Egypt was built. In the centuries that followed, some stones were added and some were moved. About 3,500 years ago, Stonehenge was finally done changing.

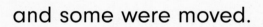

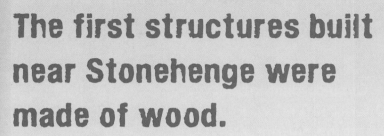
The first structures built near Stonehenge were made of wood.

The first man-made structures near the Stonehenge site were made out of wooden posts. These were put up about 5,000 years before the first stones arrived. Some people think they might have been totem poles, similar to those made by Native Americans of northwestern North America.

Stonehenge Timeline

As we've seen, Stonehenge has a very long history. Here are some key dates and events in its construction.

3100 BC

Circular ditch about 360 feet (110 m) wide is dug at the current site.

2600 BC

Bluestones, originally placed at the edge of the area, are moved to where many of the wooden posts had once been.

3000 BC

Holes are dug in the circle for wooden posts. Stonehenge is used as a graveyard.

8000 BC

Four large pine posts nearly 3 feet (0.9 m) wide are erected near the current site.

2600 BC to 2400 BC

Thirty huge sarsen stones are erected to form an outer circle. Inside the circle, more sarsens form a horseshoe pattern.

2280 BC to 1930 BC

Smaller bluestones are rearranged to form a circle in between the sarsen stones.

1550 BC

More holes are dug around the outer sarsen circle. This is the last known change made to Stonehenge.

1930 BC to 1600 BC

Bluestones are moved again to match the inner horseshoe pattern of the sarsen stones.

FACT 13

There are a few wild theories about how Stonehenge was built.

Some say it would have been too hard for ancient people to build Stonehenge without help. One **theory** says aliens from other worlds visited Earth. These aliens could have shared their knowledge and taught ancient humans how to build such an impressive monument.

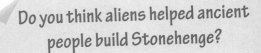

Do you think aliens helped ancient people build Stonehenge?

The people who created Stonehenge were some of the earliest known astronomers.

Stonehenge was built so it lines up with the sun on the longest and shortest days of the year. This tells us that the builders understood **astronomy**. Some people think Stonehenge could have been used as a calendar to mark holidays or ceremonies.

Tall Stones, Tall Tales

Some legends say the wizard Merlin built Stonehenge.

One popular tale says an army of 15,000 men tried but failed to move stones to build the monument. They asked the **legendary** wizard Merlin for help. Merlin used his magical powers to move the stones to Salisbury Plain and put Stonehenge together.

Merlin

In British mythology, Merlin was the personal magician of the legendary King Arthur. This painting from the 1500s shows Merlin building Stonehenge.

These remains have been named the Stonehenge archer. They were found buried in the ditch circling Stonehenge.

FACT 16

Many Stonehenge legends celebrate the stones' magical powers.

Many years ago, people may have believed Stonehenge had the power to heal. Skeletons found buried nearby show signs of illness or injury. These people may have traveled to Stonehenge seeking medical help, only to die there.

A Place of Monumental Interest

FACT 17

Graffiti thousands of years old can be found carved into the stones of Stonehenge.

Using a special laser, researchers have uncovered many secrets of Stonehenge's past—including graffiti. The markings range from a few hundred years old to thousands of years old. Much of the graffiti are dagger and ax shapes carved into the monument more than 3,000 years ago.

Sir Christopher Wren, a famous 17th-century architect, left his mark on Stonehenge.

Experts now think thousands of ancient people gathered at Stonehenge before the enormous stones were put in place to celebrate the annual winter solstice and to honor their dead.

FACT 18

Some experts now think Stonehenge was originally a graveyard for royal families.

In 2013, **archaeologists** discovered numerous graves around Stonehenge. The original positions of the bluestones marked the graves where people were buried. Experts think ancient royal families may have traveled from all over England to honor and bury their dead at Stonehenge.

A Promising Future

Each year, more than a million people from all over the world come to see Stonehenge.

Stonehenge is more popular than ever.

It gets over 1 million visitors a year.

That wasn't always the case.

"Only" about 20,000 people

visited Stonehenge in 1920.

More than 18,000 people

visited Stonehenge in one

day during the summer

solstice of 2011!

Visitors have been drawn to Stonehenge for thousands of years.

Some of the monument's stones are taller than a school bus!

FACT 20

Stonehenge will be around for a long time to come.

UNESCO is a part of the United Nations that recognizes and protects historic and cultural locations around the world. This group named Stonehenge a World **Heritage** Site in 1986. This means that Stonehenge will be protected and kept in good shape for many years to come.

Stonehenge Today

For thousands of years, Stonehenge has filled people with wonder. Who built it, and why? There's a lot we still don't know about the great monument. However, it stands as a symbol of ancient people's skill and creativity, as well as their understanding of the **cosmos**.

Thanks to efforts to preserve Stonehenge, it continues to amaze visitors. One day, you may find yourself standing next to its great standing stones, sharing the same feeling of awe that inspired ancient man to build it.

Today, a highway passes right by Stonehenge. This makes it easier for people to visit it.

Glossary

archaeologist: a scientist who studies past human life and activities

artifact: something made by humans in the past

astronomy: the science of stars, planets, and other heavenly bodies

cosmos: the universe, or everything that exists

geologist: a scientist who studies the history of Earth and its life as recorded in rocks

heritage: something handed down from the past

legendary: referring to someone or something spoken about in legends, or myths about the past

primitive: belonging to a very early time

quarry: a deep pit where stones or other materials have been dug up

solstice: the time of year when the sun is farthest north (summer solstice) or farthest south (winter solstice) of the equator

structure: something that has been built, such as a building or monument

theory: an idea formed after careful study

version: a form of something that is different from the ones that came before and after it

For More Information

Books

Aronson, Marc. *If Stones Could Speak: Unlocking the Secrets of Stonehenge.* Washington, DC: National Geographic, 2010.

McDaniel, Sean. *Stonehenge.* Minneapolis, MN: Bellwether Media, 2012.

Websites

Panoramic
www.english-heritage.org.uk/daysout/properties/stonehenge/world-heritage-site/map/panoramic/
Never been to Stonehenge? No problem! Visit this link for a virtual tour of the ancient monument. Also find a link to an interactive map.

Stonehenge, Avebury and Associated Sites
whc.unesco.org/en/list/373
Learn more about Stonehenge, as well as a nearby henge named Avebury, from the United Nations Educational, Scientific and Cultural Organization (UNESCO).

Index